THE CPD
Pocketbook

By Susan Elkin

toons:
..il ..ailstone

Published by:

Teachers'
Pocketbooks

Teachers' Pocketbooks
Laurel House, Station Approach,
Alresford, Hampshire SO24 9JH, UK
Tel: +44 (0)1962 735573
Fax: +44 (0)1962 733637
E-mail: sales@teacherspocketbooks.co.uk
Website: www.teacherspocketbooks.co.uk

*Teachers' Pocketbooks is an imprint of
Management Pocketbooks Ltd.*

Series Consultant: **Brin Best**.

This edition published 2006.

British Library Cataloguing-in-Publication
Data. A catalogue record for this book is
available from the British Library.

ISBN-13   978 1 903776 72 8
ISBN-10   1903776 72 4

Design, typesetting and graphics by Efex Ltd.
Printed in UK

Contents

Introduction

A new expectation for teachers

Learning is a lifelong process. It begins at birth and it doesn't stop until death. Life is a learning continuum. You gather information, skills and understanding as you go along.

Ongoing learning is a fact of life for everyone, but it's particularly important for teachers because they have responsibility for the learning of others. That's why CPD – Continuous Professional Development – matters so much.

In the past, CPD for teachers has been a very narrow concept. Many teachers equated it with going on courses, which can be a heavy cost to a school's low (or non-existent!) CPD budget, and not much else. Clearly, courses can be useful and some are excellent (see pages 81-82) but they are only a small part of CPD.

Then in 1988 Kenneth Baker, Education Secretary, introduced five compulsory training days a year for teachers, still often called 'Baker days'. In a way that was limiting too, but it was also the beginning of a new approach to teacher learning.

Introduction

New opportunities to develop

Suddenly there was an expectation that all teachers should go on finding new ways of doing their jobs better. Training doesn't stop when you leave college. It continues every day, week, month and year of your teaching life. Think of it as a career-long journey of discovery.

In 2005 the Teacher Training Agency (TTA) got a big new role. Re-named Training and Development Agency (TDA) it took on responsibility for the CPD of existing teachers as well as for attracting and training student teachers.

At the same time, organisations like the General Teaching Council, National College of School Leadership and Specialist Schools and Academies Trust are developing new learning opportunities for teachers. So are all the teaching unions and many other bodies. Then there are the splendid learning resources available from Teachers' TV. CPD for teachers, in all its forms, is now high on the national agenda.

Introduction

How this book can help

This book aims to:

- Show that you don't have to go on an expensive course to learn
- Encourage you to value different learning opportunities
- Give you tips and advice about different forms of CPD
- Provide information about different ways of learning to be a better teacher
- Direct you to useful organisations and sources of further information
- Inspire your CPD by sharing teachers' first hand learning experiences

What is CPD?

 CPD in Your
Own School

 Distance Learning

 Teachers' International
Professional
Development

 CPD Through
Colleagues Beyond
Your Own School

 Traditional INSET
and Courses

 Maintaining a
CPD Portfolio

 The Role
of the CPD
Coordinator

What is CPD?

Your colleagues are CPD

Learn with colleagues and let them learn with you. The teachers you work with are a free, on-site CPD source. Every teacher can tap into this resource by:

- Being mentored
- Being a mentor
- Being coached
- Being a coach
- Shadowing another teacher
- Observing in the classroom
- Being observed in the classroom

In most of these situations learning and teaching are so bound up together that you cannot split them. If you observe a colleague's lesson or shadow a teacher through the school day and discuss it with him or her afterwards you are learning together rather than one of you learning from the other.

Colleagues elsewhere are CPD

Look beyond the teachers in your own school to those in other local schools. Teachers across a consortium, federation, cluster, in a university or other less formal grouping are in a good position to help and learn from each other. You can:

- Visit other schools to observe and learn about different ways of working
- Welcome outside colleagues to your school
- Form 'talkshops' with groups of teachers from elsewhere. For instance two history departments or all the form tutors in both schools for one year could, once a term, get together to share good practice and ideas
- Become, or use the expertise of, an advanced skills teacher (see pages 64-65)
- Use the internet and video conferencing to communicate with colleagues further afield
- Take part in international exchanges (see pages 50-58)

Reading newspapers and watching TV is CPD

Keep yourself well informed about what is going on in the world of education by reading some of these publications:

- Education sections of national newspapers, especially *The Guardian* and *The Independent*, which both publish weekly education supplements
- *TES (Times Education Supplement)*
- *TSES (Times Scottish Education Supplement)*
- *THES (Times Higher Education Supplement)*

Get into the Teachers' TV habit. The channel, which is supplied digitally, runs dozens of programmes every week offering subject-based resources and information and learning for teachers along with news and features. See www.teacherstv.org.uk. You can record or 'stream' what you want to see.

Reading teacher-focused publications is CPD

- Magazines and newsletters produced by professional associations, eg NUT's *The Teacher*, ATL's *Report* or NAHT's *Leadership Focus*

- Subject association journals such as *British Journal of Teaching Physical Education* **www.pea.uk.com** or *Teaching History* **www.history.org.uk**

- *SecEd*, weekly (term time only) free newspaper published by MA Education. Sent to every secondary school (including independents) in Britain. **www.sec-ed.co.uk.** The same company produces *EYE* (Early Years Educator) and *5-7 Educator*

- Optimus Publishing – monthly newsletters. More than 12 subscription-only titles including *CPD Update*, *Education Law Update* and *Secondary Headship* **www.optimuspub.co.uk**

- Questions Publishing – subscription-only magazines including *Managing Schools* and *Citizenship* and *Teaching Thinking & Creativity* **www.education-quest.com**

- *Teaching Expertise*, subscription-only magazine devoted to CPD **www.teachingexpertise.com**

And don't forget the wealth of education updates now available online – see page 109.

Sabbaticals are CPD

And yes, they really exist. Sadly the government scheme to fund them has ended, but some lucky teachers really do get paid time away from the classroom for teacher exchange, to research, benefit from a scholarship, take a career break and/or to study.

- NUT funds a handful of CPD scholarships each year www.teachers.org.uk
- Heads and Teachers in Industry arranges and funds teacher placements in business www.hti.org.uk 024 7641 0104
- The Goldsmiths Company offers grants for innovative projects (such as a teacher who went to New Zealand to study Maori culture) www.thegoldsmiths.co.uk/education/refreshmentgrant.htm/ 020 7606 7010
- Central Bureau for Educational Visits and Exchanges (CBEVE) funds some sabbaticals. www.britishcouncil.org/cbeve 0207 389 4004, Fax 0207 389 4426
- Gatsby Teacher Fellowships pays for teachers of maths, design technology or science to undertake research www.gtf.org.uk 020 7410 7127
- Some Oxford and Cambridge Colleges offer one-term fellowships for teachers, but you have to ring round individual colleges to find out what's on offer
- Some independent schools, such as Benenden and Eton, give teachers a paid sabbatical term off, by negotiation, every ten years

Other activities are CPD too

CPD also includes:

- Writing articles and books
- Reflecting on learning and recording it
- Attending exhibitions and shows. Entry is usually free and many now run CPD seminars at very low cost
- Studying through distance learning (see pages 40-48)
- Doing research (see pages 29-37)
- Undergoing performance management
- Conducting feedback sessions with pupils: 'What did you learn from this lesson/activity?'
- Talking to colleagues informally
- Building and maintaining an individual CPD portfolio (see pages 84-90)
- Studying and discussing CPD-related books (such as this one!) in groups

CPD is all embracing

Imagine CPD is a big and exciting
umbrella. Under it comes any – yes, any –
activity through which you learn to do your job
better so that your pupils get a better education.

Think of it as a personal development tool. Anything you
learn develops you as a person as well as improving your
professional skills, knowledge and understanding. Personal and
professional development cannot really be separated.

Think of something which you thought you were learning or doing for yourself
which, as it turned out, also made you a better teacher.
Studying a foreign language? Having your own children? Visiting an historic site
or going to the theatre? Learning a new skill such as abseiling or patisserie?
Reflect on how and why it improved your teaching.

The following chapters look at different kinds of CPD in more detail and explore how
you can get the best out of them.

What is CPD?

 CPD in Your Own School ◀

 Distance Learning

 Teachers' International Professional Development

 CPD Through Colleagues Beyond Your Own School

 Traditional INSET and Courses

 Maintaining a CPD Portfolio

 The Role of the CPD Coordinator

CPD in Your Own School

Benefits of mentoring

Mentoring someone means giving advice from your own experience. Being involved in mentoring is a valuable form of CPD because it's a two-way process. Both colleagues learn.

A teacher being mentored gets:

- Advice
- Someone to bounce ideas off
- Impartial comment
- Focus on detail which might otherwise be unnoticed
- Opportunities to discuss the quality of his or her work in a professional way

Some people call the person being mentored 'a mentee'. Use it if you like it!

Benefits of being a mentor

A mentor gets:

- Insights into a colleague's work
- Opportunities to analyse and reflect on what makes good practice
- Challenge of thinking of workable suggestions to help colleague
- Chance to consider own work afresh by comparing it with a colleague's
- Time set aside for professional discussion and debate

If you are an experienced teacher, consider volunteering to mentor a less experienced colleague. There is potential for this in any school, but the most obvious opportunities arise in schools involved in School Centred Initial Teacher Training (SCITT) and/or Graduate Teacher Training Programme (GTTP). You can learn/improve mentoring skills by observing and talking to more experienced mentors.

The right mentor

Whether you are an NQT, a headteacher newly in post, or something in between, it is vital that the mentor and the person being mentored feel comfortable working together.

Both should agree to the relationship. Mentoring only works effectively as a form of CPD when both partners are committed and happy to work with, and learn from, each other.

The mentor should have:

- Appropriate experience. For example, a new head's mentor is usually a well-established head from another school or a recently retired head. An NQT's mentor is an experienced and successful teacher
- Time set aside on the school timetable to meet the person being mentored for regular, extended, in-depth discussions
- A professional manner – assertive and friendly, not authoritarian and/or over-familiar

Mentoring meetings

Hold meetings at fixed times – such as after school on Tuesdays or during period 3 on Fridays. Treat this as a serious commitment. Mentoring matters as much as your teaching or other timetabled activities.

At each meeting:

- Follow up action points from the last meeting
- Share what has gone well during the last week and decide why
- Identify something which could have been done better and work out how
- Discuss anything which is troubling the teacher being mentored on which he/she would like advice
- Agree on things to be done
- Note the content of the meeting in writing, agree it between you and file it

If you are being mentored and need emergency advice from, or to bounce an idea off, your mentor between meetings, use phone or email. Busy headteachers often support each other by talking through problems on the phone, for example.

Unofficial mentors

If you're new to teaching or to a school, there may be someone on the staff who can give you guidance and advice informally.

It's a good way of learning a lot but choose your unofficial mentor with care. Don't get involved with the staffroom cynic who has come to hate school, teachers and pupils – sadly, there's one in most schools.

– Hate it all

But someone who has been teaching a long time, who knows your pupils and the content of what you have to teach, can be an invaluable source of CPD. Talk, for instance, in a primary school to the teacher who had your class last year. At secondary level listen to colleagues who work with your pupils in different subject areas or who teach the same subject as you.

Books about mentoring

Developing as Secondary School Mentor by Alan Child & Stephen Merrill
Published by Learning Matters, 2005

The Induction and Mentoring of a Newly Qualified Teacher by Kevan Bleach
Published by David Fulton Publishers, 1999

Issues in Mentoring edited by Trevor Kerry & Ann Shelton Mayes
Published by Routledge Falmer, 1994

Mentoring in Schools by Sarah Fletcher
Published by Routledge Falmer, 2000

Mentoring Pocketbook by Geoff Alred, Bob Garvey & Richard Smith
Published by Management Pocketbooks, 1998

Teachers as Mentors by Barbara Field & Terry Field
Published by Routledge Falmer, 1994

Teachers Mentoring Teachers by John C. Daresh
Published by Paul Chapman Publishing, 2002

Coaching

Coaching is a relationship and a process in which the coach facilitates the learning of another. A coach helps people to perform better than they currently are by developing their skills and confidence.

Two people can take it in turns to coach each other, or there may be a fixed coach/'coachee' relationship.

A coach is an equal, unlike the more experienced mentor.

Like effective mentoring, coaching is based on mutual trust and partnership.

Coaches empower by asking open questions. This helps the coachee to recognise the need for change and to find ways of making it happen. Coaching promotes independent thinking. But the coachee decides what to do next. Coaching is never 'top down'.

Coaches learn to question and listen well. Their language and leadership skills develop too. (See book list on page 25.)

Being a coach

If you are a coach:

- Meet to arrange a focus. If necessary, seek permission to observe the coachee in their role, whether it's teaching a lesson or managing a department
- Agree what you will concentrate on in any observations and what will happen to any notes made
- Encourage the teacher you are working alongside to reflect on their own performance
- Use open coaching questions to draw out learning
- Revisit the classroom (or wherever) quite soon afterwards
- Reflect on improvements already happening and agree what to explore next
- Meet the teacher again for further discussion
- Repeat the process as many times as you both feel it's helpful

Classroom coaching

Some possible focuses for a coach and coachee to explore during a classroom coaching session:

- Beginning of lesson
- End of lesson
- How much opportunity pupils are given to interact
- Pacing of lesson
- Handling of resources
- Management of pupil behaviour
- Preparation of material in advance
- Teacher's body language
- Teacher's use of language to pupils
- Teacher's rapport with pupils (use of names, thanking them for contributions etc)
- Level of engagement of pupils with content of lesson
- Handling of disciplinary infringements

And don't forget that coaching, like mentoring, is a two-way process. The coach learns too.

Books about coaching

Coaching & Reflecting Pocketbook by Peter Hook, Ian McPhail & Andy Vass
Published by Teachers' Pocketbooks, 2006

Coaching in Schools by Michael Brearley
Published by Crown House Publishing, 2005

Coaching Solutions: Practical Ways to Improve Performance in Education
by Will Thomas & Alistair Smith
Published by Network Educational Press Ltd, 2004

Coaching Teachers and Teaching Assistants by Fiona Eldridge
Published by Paul Chapman Publishing, April 2006

Quality Teaching in a Culture of Coaching by Stephen G Barkley & Terri Bianco
Published by Scarecrow Publishing, 2005

Classroom observation

A teacher who watches you in the classroom can learn from you and can also give you valuable feedback on your work. Classroom observation does not involve criticism or value judgements. It is an opportunity to find out how different people manage the same material, the same students and/or the same problems. It's a constructive and supportive way in which two colleagues can enhance their CPD.

Some teachers choose to video each other in the classroom as part of observation. Some schools go still further. Brighton Hill Community College in Basingstoke in Hampshire has established 'teacher observatories.'

It means that teachers who volunteer to take part can be filmed at work and watched (by agreement) in another part of the building for CPD purposes. After the lesson teachers study the film together. The school finds this facility particularly useful for its ITT students and NQTs and for sharing expertise with the special school in its consortium.

Book recommendation: *An Introduction to Classroom Observation* by Ted Wragg, published by Routledge Falmer, 1999.

Case study

Michelle Flannery is a teacher of design and technology at Mary Hare School, a national grammar school for the deaf at Newbury in Berkshire. As an NQT she was mentored by Brian Lee, the school's head of professional development.

'I'd done my PGCE in Brighton and came to Mary Hare as its first ever NQT. I'd never lived away from home before and I was only 22, so I was very glad of the support which I got from being well mentored by someone older.

I had weekly meetings with Brian during which we talked about what had gone well and he advised me about dealing with any problems I'd had. He also looked at my lesson plans and liaised with my head of department. At the same time he arranged for some of my lessons to be observed and created a programme of observation for me so that I could learn from watching other teachers with classes.

Case study (cont'd)

And there was a most useful one-off meeting for all Newbury's NQTs and their mentors which Brian and I attended together. It was good networking for the NQTs who went on having meetings after that. I think it was also a good experience for Brian to network with other mentors because he was new to the role then, although the school has since had another NQT who followed a similar programme of mentoring.

I have done a lot of other CPD since my NQT year and I think it's partly because of the good base I gained through the mentoring. It gave me confidence.

I have taken special qualifications in teaching the deaf – obviously. I have also recently completed an MA and trained in the teaching of PSHE. Brian has encouraged me in all this, so in a way the mentoring is ongoing.

I am very happy in this school which has 210 pupils aged 11-18, many of them boarders from elsewhere in the country. Because of the mentoring, and continuing support, I feel very settled. So it helps retain staff too'

School-based research

Undertaking research in your own school or area is a good way of enhancing your CPD. You can also add to the general body of knowledge about teaching and learning.

It is usually called 'action' research because it's not theory-based.

You might want to collect and analyse evidence about say, boys' achievement in maths. Or you might be curious about the effect in your school of children's position in a family (eldest child, only boy, middle of three, etc) on attainment.

Doing research means gathering information, sometimes called 'raw data', in a planned way. For example, if you're a foundation stage teacher you might observe specific children's speech development at intervals during a school year, making detailed notes or perhaps recordings. When you have all the information you want, draw your findings together and attempt to reach some general conclusions.

Collecting information for action research

To find out what you need to know you will probably need to:

- Study documents and records (eg SATs results or school registers)
- Devise questionnaires
- Make classroom observations
- Observe pupils outside the classroom eg in the playground and around the school
- Hold interviews with teachers, pupils, parents, governors
- Read other research relating to the topic you are investigating

Recording your research findings

Write it up so that others can read about it. Your report should:

- Explain what the research set out to do
- Describe how you did it
- Come to some conclusions and/or make recommendations
- Use graphs, charts and diagrams if they make the content clearer
- Be concise
- Be written in clear jargon-free English

Spreading the word about your research

Once your research is complete you could talk to colleagues about it at an INSET session. You can also:

- Print it as a simple stapled document and circulate hard copies within your school and beyond
- Email it to schools that your school is in partnership with, locally and further afield
- Publish it on your own and/or the school's website if appropriate

Using your action research
Remember that the key benefit of action research is that what you have learned will change and improve the way you work. If, for example, you systematically observe foundation stage children at play, you will develop a better understanding of the relationship between play and learning. If you study the effectiveness of various revision techniques for GCSE history students, your knowledge will change the way you teach them in future. Action research is like a treasure trail too. It can always be revised, further developed or form a stepping stone to more research.

Getting research published in periodicals and journals

You might also consider offering your research, or an article based on it, to a specialist teachers' publication such as:

- *G&T Update* (www.optimuspub.co.uk)
- *Early Years Update* (www.optimuspub.co.uk)
- *Managing Schools Today* (www.education-quest.com)
- *Pastoral Care in Education* (www.blackwellspublishing.com)
- *Teaching Geography* (www.geography.org.uk)
- *Spoken English* (www.esbuk.org)

Search the internet for appropriate specialist journals or look in the periodicals section of your nearest university library.

Wider publication means that more teachers (and, by extension, pupils) can benefit.

More formal research

Instead of organising your own 'home-based' research you might make more formal arrangements by working with one of the organisations below:

- GTC (England) publishes Research of the Month on its website. **www.gtce.org.uk**
- Any Higher Education Institution. There is a research component in all higher degrees on education subjects
- British Educational Research Association (BERA) **www.bera.ac.uk**
- National Foundation for Educational Research (NFER) **www.nfer.ac.uk**
- TDA (Training and Development Agency, formerly Teacher Training Agency) has an expanded remit for CPD including the promotion of research – particularly through its School Based Research Consortia Initiative **www.tda.gov.uk**
- Evidence-based Education UK **www.cemcentre.org/ebeuk**
- Your LEA may have details of local research projects or of teachers wishing to start them, with whom you might collaborate

Or you might undertake action research as part of a qualification such as an MA or MEd. You will be working under the supervision of an external tutor who will help you to decide on a suitable research method.

Books to help with research

Handbook for Teacher Research by Colin Lankshear & Michele Knobel
Published by Open University Press, 2004

Research Methods in Education by Louis Cohen et al
Published by Routledge Falmer, 2000

Teacher's Guide to Classroom Research by David Hopkins
Published by Open University Press, 2002

The Art of Action Research in the Classroom by Christine Macintyre
Published by David Fulton Publishers, 2000

Case study

Gail Bedford, headteacher of Mount Pleasant Primary School at Brierley Hill in the West Midlands encourages the staff at her 425-pupil school to be systematic researchers.

'School-based research is part of our CPD programme. This often leads to innovative practice which in turn affects whole school policy.

Recently individual members of staff at Mount Pleasant have investigated:

- Factors affecting under-achievement
- The role of spoken language in communication
- Effective learning in the early years
- Encouragement of lifelong learning at an early age
- Advance learning in ICT
- Transition between key stages
- Importance of learning environment

Case study (cont'd)

Each piece of research has been of great interest and help to the teacher concerned. It has also developed the subject knowledge and management skills of these individuals. But, importantly, every piece of research has also benefited the whole school as findings were shared with colleagues. Action research is whole-school CPD.

And it can lead to unexpected further CPD. I researched the transition experience of children moving from reception to Key Stage 1. That led to an invitation to present a paper at an international conference in Australia. The DfES Innovation Unit then picked that up and now I am leading a national project called YIP-EE (Year 1 Project: Excellence Enjoyment). We are examining the tensions experienced by teachers and children as they progress to Key Stage 1.

Every school has teachers wanting answers to (often small) questions. Action research does not need to be linked to a university; neither does it have to be shared with anyone outside the school. But it can be a good way of initiating change.'

Latin proverb

By learning you will teach;
by teaching you will learn

What is CPD?

 CPD in Your
Own School

 ► Distance Learning

 Teachers' International
Professional
Development

 CPD Through
Colleagues Beyond
Your Own School

 Traditional INSET
and Courses

 Maintaining a
CPD Portfolio

 The Role
of the CPD
Coordinator

Distance Learning

Is distance learning for you?

Distance learning involves studying under the supervision of an organisation which is not local to you.

Pros:
- You can organise your study flexibly around your other commitments
- Tuition is usually cheaper than courses involving regular classes at college
- You don't have to spend time and money travelling to classes
- You can access courses from providers all over the world

Cons:
- It requires a high level of self-motivation and discipline
- You may miss the stimulation of regular contact with fellow students
- It is easy to fall behind in your studies
- Most distance learning courses have high drop-out rates

Scope of distance learning

You can use distance learning to learn almost anything: from management to dealing with head lice, or from training in school finance to dissuading parents from parking across the school gates. For instance you could:

- Update your subject knowledge to study a new curriculum area if you want to move into a new subject area

- If you're a primary teacher, get informed about, say music or science, which you may not have taken to a high level in the past

- Learn about an education topic such as gifted and talented children or assessment

- Study leadership and management issues

Distance learning opportunities

- National Open College Network. **www.noc.org.uk** runs courses from entry level to NVQ 3. Teachers could find options on art and design, managing volunteers, ICT and financial literacy useful

- International Centre for Distance Learning **www.icdl.open.ac.uk** lists 300 distance learning providers offering 5000 different courses

- Study2U **www.study2U.com** is a search engine which helps you to find distance learning courses, mostly in the US but also some in Canada, the UK and elsewhere

- Learn Direct **www.learndirect.co.uk** offers distance learning courses in computing and languages which may help some teachers

- Some of the subject organisations, such as the Geographical Association **www.geography.org.uk**, offer CPD by distance learning. (See page 108 for a list of associations)

Higher degrees by distance learning

Post-graduate courses which can be studied through online teaching; occasional weekend or holiday face-to-face tutorials; written, posted and tutor-marked assignments returned electronically or by post and which always involve individual research include:

- Master of Arts (MA)
- MBA (Master of Business Administration)
- M Ed (Master of Education)
- M Sc (Master of Science)
- PhD or DPhil (Doctor of Philosophy)
- EdD (Doctor of Education)

Modules leading towards these degrees can often be taken as stand-alones and/or counted towards various certificates and diplomas.

Many universities and institutes of education now have a distance learning arm. The highly respected Open University pioneered distance learning and is a good starting point if you are considering this way of studying:

The Open University, Walton Hall, Milton Keynes, MK7 6AA.
01908 274066 www.open.ac.uk

Organise your time

To get the best out of distance learning you need to be very systematic to take it as seriously as you would any other form of study.

Think of it as a commitment to yourself.

- Work out how much time each week the work needs and allocate blocks of time

- Aim to do the work in the evenings, at weekends, late at night, early in the mornings or when you know that you can realistically fit it in

- Think of it as a personal timetable like your school timetable. Draw a timetable plan if it helps

Organise your workplace

- Decide where you are going to work. Ideally, you need a dedicated space where you can leave your things, such as a table in a corner of the living room. Spare bedrooms, if available, are ideal for this

- You will probably also need some shelves for books and files

- You will almost certainly need a computer at your work place

- Be tidy and orderly. Keep your papers in labelled files

- Use Post-its® to mark places in books and use bookmarks on websites

- Explain to your family what you're doing and why so that they respect your study time

Contact with fellow students

Many distance learning students miss the opportunities to chat to fellow students about the learning and to bounce ideas off them.

- Consider doing a distance learning course with a partner from your own school. If two of you do the same course then you can help each other
- Use the notice boards, chat rooms and other online discussion communities which many distance learning providers set up
- Ask to be put in touch with others in your area who are doing the same course
- Make the effort to attend any face-to-face seminars which are offered as part of the course so that you meet fellow students

Case study

James Roberts is a newly appointed deputy head at Northolt High School in the London Borough of Ealing. He completed an MA in Educational Leadership and Management with the Open University in 2004.

'I was working in a referral unit for excluded pupils in the London Borough of Brent, having previously been a secondary school head of year when I started my MA. I chose distance learning because my children were then aged 7, 5 and 1 and I wanted to be at home with them and with my wife in the early evening. I was then able to do my degree work after the children were in bed. Distance learning is very family-friendly. Attending college regularly would have been far harder.

There were immediate benefits. I began in February. Reading the Study Guide and the carefully structured course materials made me instantly more analytical. So my applications for Senior Management posts were much better informed. I was appointed Assistant Head at Whitmore High School in Harrow that April and took up the post in September.

Case study (cont'd)

I have never found isolation a problem. I've always been a self-directed learner. So distance learning suits the way I am. Of course there are no lectures, but you have monthly tutorials and your tutor marks your assignments. I don't think I missed out at all and it wasn't too onerous. Being able to tailor the research aspect of the work to challenges I was facing at school in my new job was valuable too.

I am now about to start the National Professional Qualification for Headship (NPQH) and am considering a Doctorate in Education. As a deputy head I now deal with weightier whole-school matters and I think a doctorate might help.'

What is CPD?

 CPD in Your
Own School

 Distance Learning

 Teachers' International
Professional
Development

 CPD Through
Colleagues Beyond
Your Own School

 Traditional INSET
and Courses

 Maintaining a
CPD Portfolio

 The Role
of the CPD
Coordinator

Teachers' International Professional Development

Why TIPD?

Every country in the world has its own unique education system. Some, of course, are more developed than others.

Visiting schools and working with teachers overseas is an excellent way of:

- Finding out how others do things
- Learning from schools different from your own
- Sharing your own expertise
- Learning how to see your own teaching in a wider context
- Acquiring learning which you can pass on when you're back in the UK so that the CPD benefits are extended
- Having experiences which you can share with your pupils
- Finding opportunities for establishing links between your school in the UK and the overseas one which can lead to video-conferencing, exchanging emails and pupil visits

Where and what

Working with a colleague in another country benefits your own teaching and it might get you a trip to, say, Russia, Australia or Hong Kong. Teachers International Professional Development (TIPD) is always regarded as a two-way process – all the teachers involved learn from each other. It includes:

- Organising pupil exchanges with schools in other countries, as many modern languages departments do. Pupils and staff usually stay in the homes of students and teachers from the other school

- Teacher exchange. You teach abroad for a term or a year while the teacher you're replacing works in your place in Britain. Sometimes exchangers use each other's homes and cars too. **www.britishcouncil.org/learning-ie-teaching-exchange.htm**

- Short trips funded through the government's TIPD scheme are managed by the Specialist Schools and Academies Trust **www.specialistschool.org.uk/tipd**, British Council **www.britishcouncil.org/tipd**, League of Exchange of Commonwealth Teachers **www.lect.org.uk** and Best Practice Network **www.bestpracticenet.co.uk**

Different sorts of TIPD

Some TIPD is for individuals. Some is thematic and for groups. For example, some teachers from Gloucestershire LEA went to Hungary in 2002 to study alternative ways of handling vocational education and, in 2004, a group from the London Borough of Greenwich visited Texas to learn about behaviour management.

TIPD possibilities:

- Taking time out to work in schools abroad through Voluntary Service Overseas (VSO) which needs teachers prepared to learn by giving their skills, usually for two years, in areas in need **www.vso.org.uk**
- Spending one summer holiday working in a school in Africa through Link's Global Teachers Programme (see page 55) **www.lcd.org.uk**
- Video conferencing with schools and teachers in other countries and setting up email links – the 21st century answer to 'pen pals'!

TIPD via Specialist Schools and Academies Trust

Government funding has been available for TIPD since 2000. More than 8,000 teachers have enhanced their CPD in, for example, South Africa, USA, Australia, Hong Kong, France, Sweden and Hungary. The Specialist Schools and Academies Trust administers the scheme for the DfES, but applicants can be from any state school – primary or secondary. Eligibility is *not* restricted to specialist schools.

There are 300 places per year for short-term study visits. These are international visits on a chosen theme (such as personalised learning or inclusion). Applicants do not choose the destination.

School-determined visits involve travelling to a partner school abroad to look at an approved theme (such as citizenship or behaviour management). 500 places are available each year. Grants cover travel to the destination from a UK airport, travel insurance, accommodation, daily breakfast and dinner and necessary travel at the destination.

For further information see **www.specialistschools.org.uk/tipd**   01733 758030.

TIPD via LECT

LECT stands for the League for the Exchange of Commonwealth Teachers which organises group CPD study trips overseas for teachers. For example:

- Early years teachers to Denmark to compare approaches and meet educators, policy makers and academics (one week August 2005)
- Primary and secondary teachers to Estonia for school visits and meetings to study and compare approaches to gifted and talented education (one week October 2005)
- Primary and secondary maths and science teachers to Mumbai to study India's excellence in IT, maths and science set against the challenges faced by an historically poor country trying to make good quality education accessible to all (one week February 2006)

Because LECT participants travel in a group, and have a shared focus for the visit, they can explore ideas and best practice with colleagues. So they experience, reflect, discuss, analyse and learn as they go along.

Grants of £500-£1500 are available. **www.lect.org.uk**

Other organisations offering TIPD

- Link Community Development **www.lcd.org.uk** places a group of 'Global Teachers' in Uganda (primary) and South Africa (secondary) each summer for a four-week placement. Participants stay in the homes of African teachers or school governors and teach in the schools they're assigned to. There's extensive training and follow-up

- VSO **www.vso.org.uk** provides opportunities for teachers to recharge their batteries by taking 'time out' from teaching in Britain to work abroad in a voluntary capacity. It is campaigning for sabbatical entitlements so that more teachers can take part

- British Council **www.britishcouncil.org/learning-professional-development.htm** runs various programmes which take teachers abroad for CPD. These include:
  – Socrates programme which places teachers in Europe
  – Fulbright programme which arranges exchanges for headteachers and senior managers with the USA
  – Teacher Exchange Europe which organises exchanges with France, Spain and Germany for Modern Foreign Language teachers

- International Placements of Headteachers which is funded by National College for School Leadership **www.ncsl.org.uk**

How to get the best out of TIPD

- Go with an open mind
- Ask questions
- Observe what you see as closely as you can. One early years teacher returned from China with a startling insight into potty training, having observed Chinese families with their toddlers
- Share your knowledge but remember you don't have all the answers
- Be adaptable. One teacher stayed with the family of a teacher in Ghana and ate grubs. When in Rome . . .
- Take every opportunity to talk to teachers and pupils in your destination
- Remember that your hosts want to learn as much from you as you do from them
- Team-teach with colleagues in a destination school if you get the chance. It has a lot to show you about teaching and learning styles
- Write up your notes/thoughts/ideas every day, otherwise you will quickly forget some of your impressions
- Try to build lasting partnerships and friendships which you can develop when you're back in your own school
- Share your learning with colleagues and pupils in the UK

Case study

Chris Rolph, then deputy principal, and now principal, of Monks' Dyke Technology College, an 11-18 secondary school in Louth, Lincolnshire went to Melbourne, Australia in 2002 with a group of colleagues for TIPD purposes.

'Once over our jetlag, we began a hectic itinerary, visiting two primary schools, four secondaries, the State of Victoria's Department of Education and Training – equivalent to our DfES – and the DET's Eastern Metropolitan Region – equivalent to our LEA.

Nothing was too much trouble for our hosts. They were patient as we learnt their educational jargon and effusive when describing their initiatives and developments.

At the end of each long day we retired to a conference room in our hotel to summarise the main points, and then subdivide positive learning aspects into three groups:

- Things we could not currently afford to do
- Things we could implement in the near future
- Things we could start doing straight away

Case study (cont'd)

Examining education in another country and culture makes you take a step back and widen your field of vision. We all need to do this more when evaluating the performance of our home institutions. That's particularly pertinent to those considering developing their career into senior management, and for me in particular, as I was appointed headteacher just six days before leaving England!

The trip made a deep impression on us all and it had an immediate impact on our work. We returned with lots of positive ideas from all sorts of different places and were itching to try some of them out. There's also much that we didn't have time to do, so some of us would like to go back. That in itself is testimony to the impact of the experience on our professional lives.'

What is CPD?

 CPD in Your
Own School

 Distance Learning

 Teachers' International
Professional
Development

 CPD Through
Colleagues Beyond
Your Own School

 Traditional INSET
and Courses

 Maintaining a
CPD Portfolio

 The Role
of the CPD
Coordinator

CPD Through Colleagues Beyond Your Own School

Specialist schools

At the time of writing (2006) over two thirds of all the secondary schools in England have specialist status. The aim is for all schools to specialise. The 10 specialisms are:

- Technology
- Arts
- Music
- Humanities
- Science

- Business and enterprise
- Language
- Sport
- Maths and computing
- Engineering

Many schools are now adopting joint specialisms such as sports/music or engineering/humanities. Schools may also now take special educational needs (SEN) as an additional specialism.

Specialist schools are required to work closely with other local schools as a condition of their extra funding. Because of their specialist expertise these schools are a good source of CPD.

Learning with colleagues in specialist schools

Teachers in both primary and secondary schools might:

- Organise information-sharing meetings with specialist school colleagues
- Visit the specialist school with pupils for specialist teaching
- Team-teach with specialist school colleagues – both in your school and theirs
- Work on curriculum planning with specialist school colleagues
- Welcome specialist school colleagues to show how things are done in your school
- Borrow and share specialist resources such as a sports hall and learn new teaching skills to make the best use of them

List every specialist school in your area and its specialism. Do you have contacts at each of them? If not arrange to make contact and to meet as soon as possible. Draw up a wish-list of what you hope to learn (and what learning of your own you can share) through the link. Take your list to the meeting.

Building bridges

The two sectors – independent and maintained – have much to learn from each other by working together. The government funds dozens of 'Building Bridges' partnership projects such as:

- Eton College working with Berkshire schools to develop music teaching
- Loughborough Grammar School running maths master classes for local primary school children and organising related training conferences for their teachers
- Durham High School for Girls developing Year 6 science workshops with a cluster of primary schools in County Durham and the Education Action Zone of Easington & Peterlee. All the teachers involved widened their knowledge of key stages outside those in which they normally work
- Ashton-on-Mersey School (a state comprehensive) working with Witherslack Hall School (an independent special school) on behaviour management training, anti-bullying policies and other staff training, especially through sport

Building bridges

There have also been informal (unfunded) projects such as Benenden School in Kent working with Forest Gate Community School in the London Borough of Newham on GCSE revision courses for Year 11 and staff development for Benenden teachers who learned a great deal, especially about behaviour management, from Forest Gate staff.

Could you work with, learn from and share learning with colleagues in a school in your area which is in a different sector from yours?
Visit **www.dfes.uk/buildingbridges**

There is also scope for different sorts of state school to work in partnership. Sittingbourne Community College in Kent runs Saturday a.m. sessions for pupils from Years 5-9. It links the college with various rural feeder primaries and benefits the CPD of all staff involved.

Advanced skills teachers

The role of advanced skills teacher (AST) was devised as a CPD resource. An AST, who is paid a special allowance, has the equivalent of one day per week free from the timetable of his or her own school.

The time is spent working with his or her own colleagues, or visiting other schools and working with colleagues there, to build up expertise, usually in specialist subjects. For example AST John Stone is Head of Music at St John's Catholic Comprehensive School, Gravesend. He uses his AST time to visit local primary schools where he helps class teachers to develop specialist music teaching and learning. Staff in those schools are learning music teaching skills from John and he, in turn, is learning about the work of the schools which feed pupils into St John's.

As with so much CPD it's a two-way process. The AST is both teacher and learner. So is the receiver of AST support.

What an AST does

An AST's non-contact time can be spent:
- Producing high quality teaching materials
- Disseminating materials relating to best practice and educational research
- Providing 'model' lessons to a whole class, or a target group of pupils – eg gifted and talented, SEN, English as an acquired language etc, with staff observing
- Supporting a subject leader, eg with schemes of work, policies or management skills
- Observing lessons and advising other teachers on classroom organisation, lesson planning and teaching methods
- Helping teachers who are experiencing difficulties
- Participating in the induction and mentoring of newly qualified teachers
- Leading professional learning groups
- Supporting professional development

(Source: DfES website)

Could you enhance your CPD by becoming, or working with, an AST?
See **www.standards.dfes.gov.uk/ast/**

Federated schools

A federation is a formal link, often under a single governing body, between two or more schools. Usually the successful 'lead' school shares expertise with the less successful partner(s) in the federation. Each school has its own headteacher. For example, the successful Ninestiles Technology College in Birmingham is federated with Waverley School and International School. Haberdashers' Aske's Hatcham College, a very successful school in New Cross in South London, is federated with Haberdashers' Aske's Knight's Academy in nearby Downham on the site of the former Malory School.

Teachers in federations are in a strong position to learn from each other. They can:

- Hold department meetings across both/all schools
- Share ideas, resources and curriculum materials
- Share INSET

CPD through informal partnerships

Take every opportunity to learn with, through and from your colleagues everywhere:

- Establish links with university initial teacher training departments. It can bring invitations to help train teachers by delivering sessions (lectures, workshops etc) as well as mentoring opportunities. It's also a good way of keeping up to date with current trends and developments
- Network, perhaps by email and/or through half-termly face-to-face meetings with your opposite number in another school. So both heads of history, KS 2 coordinators or deputy heads – for instance – work together
- Set up a local discussion group with fellow 'students' in other local schools if you are undertaking distance learning
- Devise shared action research projects with colleagues in other schools
- Form a reading group which meets, say once a term, to discuss recent publications
- Tap into any expertise which you learn is in another school but which you don't have in yours, eg if the other school has a fine science specialist which you lack in your primary school, invite him/her to your school to share ideas or to lead some training

Learning from expert visitors

When outsiders visit schools it's usually to work with students but teachers working alongside them can learn a lot too. All the following visitors are valuable sources of CPD because you can watch the way they inspire pupils:

- Industry manager in connection with enterprise days etc
- Poet
- Doctor
- Charity representative
- Elderly person with memories (eg fighter pilot)
- Musician
- Storyteller
- Actor(s)
- Examiners (eg GCSE)
- Scientist
- Painter
- Athlete
- Journalist
- Religious leader
- Native speaker of a language pupils are learning

Case study

Gary Smith is head of Market Field Special School for Children with Learning Difficulties in Colchester in Essex. He and his colleagues work closely with teachers in local mainstream primary and secondary schools.

'Working with other schools is always a two-way street. They learn and so do we. For example, we have trainee teachers here on placement. Although they are specialising in special needs, and intend to work in special schools, they must also have mainstream experience during their training. That means that we work with the Initial Teacher Training Coordinator from other schools to manage these joint placements. Talking and observing means that that we all learn more about each other's work.

And often that initial contact leads to other CPD opportunities. We get a lot of requests for visits from special needs coordinators (SENCOs) and learning support assistants working with SEN pupils in those other schools, for instance. They both learn and share their own expertise in our school. Then they pass on or 'cascade' information and learning to their colleagues back in their own schools. There's a lot of co-operation and growing mutual understanding in all this.

Case study (cont'd)

The other way in which we're involved in collaborative CPD is through our expertise in autism. We have a number of autistic pupils here and, because the incidence of autism is rising, so do mainstream schools. We help with training and resources which are generally pretty scarce. To take a very simple example, an autistic child often needs a visual timetable and we can show mainstream colleagues how to provide it.

We are currently under pressure from our LEA to do even more outreach, and although funding that is a big problem, experience shows that there would be staff CPD benefits.'

What is CPD?

 CPD in Your Own School

 Distance Learning

 Teachers' International Professional Development

 CPD Through Colleagues Beyond Your Own School

 Traditional INSET and Courses

 Maintaining a CPD Portfolio

 The Role of the CPD Coordinator

Traditional INSET and Courses

INSET days

INSET, or in-service training, mostly takes place on designated days when the pupils are absent, usually five times a year. Training may consist of:

- Presentation by an outside speaker on a topic of interest to whole staff, eg health and safety, usually with activities, etc
- Training led for whole staff by one or more of the school's own staff, eg gifted and talented coordinator
- Development work such as curriculum planning undertaken in departments or other groups. This can include, for example, a group going out to learn together such as the English department visiting The Globe Theatre or all the Year 5 teachers checking out a residential centre
- Joining with another school/schools to share a prestigious (costly!) speaker

Although some have been closed in recent years, some LEAs still maintain a Professional Development Centre (PDC) for hire by schools. It can provide a well resourced INSET venue away from the teachers' schools. Most PDCs are now also let to other organisations as well as schools to offset running costs.

Pros and cons of INSET days

Pros:

- Research shows that teachers' learning is more effective if a group of colleagues has collaborated and can implement it together afterwards
- Cost of speaker quite modest if the fee is regarded as shared by the whole staff (eg £500 fee between 100 staff. Only £5 per head from the CPD budget)

Cons:

- Rare for everyone on a staff to have identical training needs, so chosen INSET unlikely to be suitable for everyone
- Staff, understandably, can get resentful at wasted time if a speaker is sub-standard or content is unsuitable
- Some teachers feel it isn't 'proper' training if they've only sat in their own school hall. Can be seen as lacking the prestige of an 'off-site' course

How to get the best out of an INSET day

Ideally all colleagues should be consulted about, and involved in, the planning of a whole-school INSET day. Then people don't feel that the training is being imposed on them and everyone feels committed. Unfortunately, because schools are (often) large and busy places, it isn't always quite like that in practice. So:

- Once you know the topic for the day, prepare – read relevant articles, use the internet

- On the day, be as positive as you can. See it as a useful learning opportunity. It's all too easy for some colleagues to be negative about INSET days and few things are as infectious as negativity. Remember, effective training doesn't necessarily tell you anything you didn't know before. It makes you think about it in a new way

- Involve yourself in the learning. Make notes, ask questions and join in the discussion

- Don't file away your INSET notes and forget about them at the end of the day! As soon as possible after the session make a list of action points – things you can use in your teaching and/or role in the school. Make sure you revisit your learning and act upon your identified action points. (Remember: the 'C' in CPD stands for 'continuing')

Helping to deliver an INSET day

Sometimes INSET is led by teachers who have, perhaps, attended an external course, conducted research or developed some form of expertise or working method which could benefit colleagues. Arguably it is more nerve-racking to face your own colleagues than it is to stand before a class of pupils or to 'teach' unknown adults.

- Prepare your session very carefully
- Have too much material rather than too little – you can always cut it as you go along
- Build in interactive sessions when colleagues work in groups or contribute to discussion so that no one sits passively listening for too long
- Use prompt cards and an overhead projector or PowerPoint
- Check numbers in advance and make sure you have enough copies of handouts
- Afterwards, make notes on what went well and what didn't so that you can adapt your technique for next time

Remember you are probably getting as much (or more) CPD out of this as anyone else present. And if word gets round of how good you are you may find yourself leading INSET for colleagues in another school or at a Professional Development Centre.

External courses

LEAs and examination boards run many courses on pastoral, management, academic and whole-school issues for teachers. So do commercial providers such as:

- ChristopherSwann.com Professional Development, Suite 408-10, The Corn Exchange, Fenwick Street, Liverpool L2 7QS; 0845 125 9010; **www.christopherswann.com**
- Mill Wharf Training and Consultancy Services, Mill Wharf, Mill Street, Birmingham, B6 4BU; 0121 628 2910; **www.mill-wharf-training.co.uk**
- Creative Education, 89 Sanderstead Road, South Croydon, Surrey CR2 0PF; 020 8666 0234; **www.creativeeducation.co.uk**
- SfE Ltd, 1 Portland Square, Bristol BS2 8RR; 0117 983 8800; **www.sfe.co.uk**
- Network Training, Mitre House, Tower Street, Taunton, Somerset TA1 4BH; 01823 353 354; **www.network-training.ac.uk**

The companies above are examples not recommendations. There are many more.

External courses

Pros:
- It's good for a teacher to get right away from the workplace to learn and reflect
- Networking with other teachers from a wide range of schools, sometimes from different parts of the country, can lead to learning and new contacts
- Teachers can acquire very specific information such as syllabus changes and how to manage them, on a course run by an examination board, or changes in the law such as the Disability Discrimination Act

Cons:
- External, commercially run or LEA courses typically are relatively expensive
- May be poor quality because the industry is unregulated. Dr Sandra Leaton Gray of the University of Cambridge, who researched *An Enquiry into Continuing Professional Development for Teachers,* told TES (April 29 2005) that 'two thirds of the continuing professional development teachers get is probably rubbish'
- Supply cover has to be arranged and funded for a teacher attending a course
- Pupils may suffer if their regular teacher is out of school too often
- Even if you're inspired by a course it can be difficult to enthuse colleagues and bring about change back at school

How to choose an external course

Study carefully the advertising material put out by providers. Look for a course which:

- Meets your precise need – such as how to get Key Stage 3 boys using the school library or how to make the best use of circle time in reception classes
- Doesn't make vague promises, eg 'will develop your management skills at any level'
- Is led by experienced practitioners such as recently retired heads or practising teachers
- Includes all handouts and refreshments so that you don't end up with a bill for extras
- Is presented by a reputable organisation which has been used by other teachers known to you

Looking elsewhere for CPD

Don't overlook museums, art galleries, charities, sports clubs, theatres, orchestras, special interest organisations and public bodies. Many offer CPD to help teachers learn to make the best use of their facilities and expertise.

Usually this is much cheaper than the CPD offered by for-profit companies. And sometimes there is no charge at all.

Many such organisations put on courses or practical training sessions for teachers. Others send advisers into schools to work with the teacher and or pupils.

Either way it's an excellent – often unrecognised and undervalued – source of teacher learning.

Examples of organisations offering teachers' CPD

The following all have well-developed education departments and affordable – or free – CPD opportunities for teachers. But be prepared to search. These few are just the tip of the iceberg:

- Dulwich Picture Gallery, London SE21 **www.dulwichpicturegallery.org.uk**
- Royal Horticultural Society, Surrey **www.rhs.org.uk**
- Fulham Football Club **www.fulhamfc.com**
- English Heritage **www.english-heritage.org.uk**
- Voluntary Service Overseas **www.vso.org.uk**
- The National Museum and Gallery, Cardiff **www.nmgw/ac.uk/nmgw/**
- Museum of Science and Industry, Manchester **www.nmsi.ac.uk/**
- Royal National Theatre **www.nationaltheatre.org.uk/education**
- Oxfam **www.oxfam.org.uk**
- Royal Society for Prevention of Cruelty to Animals **www.rspca.org.uk**
- London Symphony Orchestra **www.lso.co.uk/lsodiscovery/**

Case study

Steve Fuller is head of RE and professional mentor for Initial Teacher Training at St Wilfrid's C of E High School and Technology College, Blackburn. He attended a one-day course on stretching gifted and talented pupils in RE.

'The course was held in Manchester, which is about an hour's journey from where I live. I was impressed by the way the course was organised and planned as a forum. We had small group discussions and sessions for the whole group which consisted of about 18 people. The informal discussion with fellow RE teachers between sessions was useful too.

There was a wealth of good ideas which we were able to try out on each other in the small groups and which I found were immediately usable back in school. It was all very practical.

Case study (cont'd)

I was in the process of rewriting our schemes of work for GCSE and what I learned on the course meant that I could incorporate more ideas for differentiation and for extending very able students in mixed ability groups. Although we have had no exam results yet, we have already noticed, in just a few weeks, a clear improvement in the level of students' engagement because of the new ways of working.

I get sent a lot of bumf about courses and am doubtful about the value of some of them, but as a piece of CPD which impacts directly on pupils this course was certainly good value for money.'

What is CPD?

 CPD in Your
Own School

 Distance Learning

 Teachers' International
Professional
Development

 CPD Through
Colleagues Beyond
Your Own School

 Traditional INSET
and Courses

 Maintaining a
CPD Portfolio

 The Role
of the CPD
Coordinator

Maintaining a CPD Portfolio

Why do you need a portfolio?

If you've done it, value it. Keep an ongoing record of all aspects of your CPD. Do it electronically (known as an 'e-portfolio') or simply put it in a ring binder.

Not only will it enhance your self-esteem, it can be used for performance management or in job interviews. And putting it together will make you reflect on what you've done and learned – which is a form of CPD in itself.

Prune and update your portfolio regularly. New activities and achievements should continually supersede and supplant work done longer ago.

It is, in effect, a teacher's version of the student's Record of Achievement.

What to put in your portfolio

Include in your portfolio:

- Degree and other certificates
- Attendance certificates for courses
- Notes on courses
- Record of mentoring or being mentored
- Record of coaching or being coached
- Classroom observation notes
- Research undertaken
- Visual evidence (photographs, film etc) of projects
- Samples of student work if relevant
- Record of reading – books, etc on education topics
- Any other evidence of your learning
- Personal development activities (such as running a marathon) which have enhanced your teaching
- Record of performance management assessments

CPD portfolios for NQTs

For a newly qualified teacher the portfolio is a valuable way of demonstrating learning and meeting the induction standards to achieve Qualified Teacher Status (QTS).

All NQTs have an individualised programme of support and a designated induction tutor. They teach a slightly lighter timetable than their QTS colleagues. Time thus freed must be used to observe more experienced teachers in different settings.

Keeping a detailed portfolio is an ideal way of recording and reflecting on such observations in preparation for the (required) half-termly meeting with the induction tutor.

Some NQTs will want also to use the DfES's online support tool 'Professional and Career Development' which includes an e-portfolio incorporating a CV
www.teachernet.gov.uk/professionaldevelopment/nqt/induction

CPD portfolios for seasoned teachers

You are never too old or experienced to value your learning.
Include in your portfolio:

- Comments on mentoring less experienced colleagues as a CPD experience for you
- What you've learned from writing documents on behalf of the school such as preparing the bid for specialist school status
- Reflections on what you have learned by interviewing prospective new staff
- Being a team leader such as head of year or careers manager and the learning you have acquired from your role
- Applying for senior posts and anything you may have learned from it
- Your changing relationship with students and their learning. It's different after you have been teaching a few years from how it was when you started in the profession

Try to see everything that you do in your job
as having a CPD dimension.

Using your portfolio

If you keep your portfolio up to date and looking smart you might use it:

- To remind yourself what a lot you've achieved at those (inevitable if only occasional) times when you're feeling less than positive about yourself and your job
- As evidence and a starting point for discussion between you and the person leading your regular performance management interview
- As an indication of what you can do when you are applying for a promotion (or other job) beyond your own school
- In peer discussion with a colleague when you might look at and discuss each other's portfolio as part of a shared CPD exercise
- As a record for posterity – for yourself in retirement and for your family – of how you developed during your career

Case study

Donna McPherson is art and cross-curricular coordinator at St Martin's Primary School, Dover, Kent. Now in her fourth year of teaching she has maintained a CPD portfolio since she began, in a different school, as an NQT.

'I was advised to build a CPD portfolio four years ago and I have done so ever since. I use a ring binder.

I file in it an account of every course I attend. In both the schools I've worked in we've been required to give a written review of each course to the CPD coordinator – so it's a simple matter also to file a copy in my portfolio. I organise it in sections such as subjects like English, maths, science and so on and under headings such as behaviour. I find that there is an ongoing need to create more sections as my experience grows.

Case study (cont'd)

At the same time I record staff meetings, advice and targets set. This was especially important and relevant during my NQT year when I was involved in regular discussions about my progress and development. And during that first year I was also completing a Masters degree which I'd begun at college so the CPD log for that went in the folder too.

I also keep copies of assessment records in my portfolio. Data about tests, rising reading and spelling ages, SATs results and so on is evidence of what I have done for the children in my classes.

I find the portfolio a useful record because looking at it makes me reflect on what I've done and what I need to do. In a sense the portfolio is itself a source of CPD.

I expect it to play an important role when I reach threshold assessment because it shows my learning and development very clearly.'

What is CPD?

 CPD in Your
Own School

 Distance Learning

 Teacher's International
Professional
Development

 CPD Through
Colleagues Beyond
Your Own School

 Traditional
INSET and Courses

 Maintaining a CPD
Portfolio

 The Role
of the CPD
Coordinator

The Role of the CPD Coordinator

Who is the CPD coordinator?

The role of school CPD coordinator is a relatively new one. It has developed in parallel with CPD.

In secondary schools coordinating CPD tends to be part of an assistant or deputy head's role. In primary schools it may fall to the deputy head or, in a small school, the head.

But in any school the CPD coordinator is sometimes a teacher without other management responsibilities and for whom the role is part of his/her own professional development. It can be useful preparation for future posts such as deputy headship (Personnel).

The CPD coordinator has an overview of the training needs of all staff and matches those needs with opportunities. That usually involves managing and making the best possible use of the budget.

The CPD budget

Much CPD, as the various sections of this book have shown, costs nothing except will and effort. But attending courses, bringing in speakers and some other forms of CPD cost money. So does supply cover if a CPD activity necessitates it.

Dr Sandra Leaton Gray of University of Cambridge, who researched *An Enquiry into Continuing Professional Development for Teachers*, published April 2005, found that schools' CPD annual budgets range from £600 to £30,000. At present there are no rules about how much of its overall budget a school must spend on CPD.

Many secondary schools delegate part of the CPD budget to subject leaders to spend on colleagues' subject-specific CPD.

Managing the CPD budget

The size of a school's CPD budget is often a measure of its commitment to CPD. Small primaries, however, with very small overall budgets, are bound to have difficulty allocating a sizeable sum to staff development. Such schools have to look for tightly cost-effective ways of learning.

If you are the CPD coordinator:

- Negotiate for as large a sum as you can
- Consider raising supplementary money for CPD from sources other than the school budget, such as sponsorship
- Accept that, in a large school, only a small number of staff can attend external courses in any one year
- Look for economies such as sharing bought-in speakers with other schools

Identifying individual CPD needs

Conduct an annual audit of colleagues' training needs by circulating a questionnaire on paper or by email. The results will inform the school development plan.

Ask colleagues:

- What CPD they have undergone in the last 12 months
- What they would like to be trained in or to improve at during the next 12 months
- What ideas they have for whole school INSET

Liaise with staff responsible for performance management. Their interviews will identify CPD needs.

So, on occasion, will capability or disciplinary proceedings. CPD must be offered to help the individual to correct shortcomings or weaknesses.

Identifying wider needs

Be aware of the school's needs.

For example, if you are in a primary school whose SENCO (special educational needs coordinator) is leaving at the end of the year the school will need to train/develop someone else for the role.

As CPD coordinator you may, with the head, be involved in selecting a suitable person and you will certainly have to help plan and oversee his/her training.

Or suppose an Ofsted inspection had highlighted the need for more attention to differentiated learning across the school. It would be part of the CPD coordinator's role to facilitate some whole-school development work and budget for it.

Circulating information

CPD coordinators receive large numbers of fliers from course providers almost daily. They will also be sent information about CPD opportunities by email.

First, throw away (or delete if it's electronic) anything which cannot relate to your school, such as a conference about raising boys' achievement if you're in an all girls' school. Do it scrupulously as it comes in. Do not hoard piles of paper which will never be useful.

Then circulate subject- or interest-specific fliers to subject or other leaders, managers and coordinators. Match other more generic fliers (eg 'Managing a Key Stage' or 'Being a Coordinator') to the individuals who have identified specific training needs or wishes in their annual questionnaires. Make it clear that there are no guarantees for attendance. People will have to make a good case for a slice of your limited budget.

Display posters and fliers publicising exhibitions such as the BETT Show at Olympia in January and the Education Show at NEC, Birmingham in March. Encourage colleagues to attend. Can you negotiate cover for a half or whole day for attendees?

Sharing other information

If your school subscribes to any of the paid-for sources of CPD information listed on page 11 then circulate relevant pages and sections to colleagues who need the information. *CPD Update*, for example, freely allows subscribers to photocopy and circulate within their own institutions.

Make sure that you share anything you have found via websites or through reading which could help colleagues' learning too.

Part of your job is to be a CPD librarian. Aim to be as informative and open as you can.

Investors in People

Investors in People (IiP) is a national Standard that sets a level of good practice for the training and development of people. The Standard is widely respected as a badge of quality. It was originally designed and launched in 1995 to help successful companies to harness training and development to meet their business goals.

Since 1999 the government has been actively encouraging schools to undertake IiP as a way of ensuring that they meet the CPD needs of every one of the staff – not just teachers. It involves finding gaps in a staff's CPD and rectifying them. Training policy and practice are scrutinised and staff interviewed by external assessors before the award is made. Sometimes organisations are told that they haven't yet reached the required standard. Then they have to do more work before reapplying.

The government began actively encouraging schools to use IiP in 1999. Over half of all British schools now have IiP accreditation which has to be regularly renewed and updated. If your school isn't already signed up, it's worth investigating IiP as a means of extending CPD.
www.iipuk.co.uk; www.standards.dfes.gov.uk/sie/si/SfCC/goodpractice/iip/

Managing an INSET day – Step 1

The Head and/or leadership team will probably have decided on a topic: child protection or behaviour management, for example.

Find a good INSET leader by:

* Asking colleagues in other schools for recommendations
* Contacting relevant organisations
* Using contacts of colleagues and governors at your own school
* Approaching one of the INSET providing companies who offer course leaders to visit schools

Managing an INSET day – Step 2

Liaise in detail with the course leader.

- What equipment does she or he need?
- What preparation should colleagues do?
- What format will the session take?
- What room/seating arrangements are needed?
- Does the speaker need guidance about transport, location or accommodation?

Organise refreshments with the catering staff. Be precise about what you need and when and for how many people.

Make sure that every colleague has an individual copy of the day's timings and arrangements. There will always be someone who says that she or he didn't know what was going on if you just put a notice on a notice board.

A personal development INSET day

Consider using your colleagues' extracurricular interests and talents to run an occasional INSET day on which teachers can learn from each other about things which are not directly related to teaching. It helps morale and is refreshing. It also makes colleagues feel valued, which can improve their teaching.

It shows teachers how others present and explain things too – a useful form of CPD.

Ask what people can offer. Then organise four or five workshops which run simultaneously on the INSET day. If you run the whole programme twice colleagues can opt into two different sessions.

Shown right is a sample timetable for a personal development INSET day.

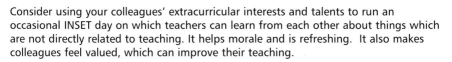

Timetable

10.00-12.30	Workshops A, B, C, D and E
12.30	lunch
1.30-4.00	Workshops A, B, C, D and E

Each person can choose one workshop in each session

Examples of personal development topics

I organised INSET days of this sort including teacher-run workshops on:

- Tai Chi
- Calligraphy
- Music appreciation
- Van Gogh
- Time management
- Chaos theory
- Introduction to Spanish
- Basic embroidery
- Managing your money
- Folk dancing
- English wine

Your colleagues may surprise you!

Case study

Steve Jones is assistant head at Bartley Green School, a specialist technology and sports college in Birmingham. His responsibilities include the coordination of CPD.

'As well as co-ordinating CPD provision across the school, my job involves managing the induction of NQTs. That includes setting objectives, monitoring and reporting progress as well as organising their training provision both in-house and from external sources. I look after the induction of new staff too and I coordinate initial teacher training (ITT) in school.

I am also responsible for writing the CPD development plan and I liaise with the Support Services Manger about CPD for support staff. Then there's Performance Management, the structure of which I review annually.

I also represent the school on various bodies including Southwest area network of schools (SWAN) and Oaks Collegiate, both of which deliver CPD activities. We're involved in the Graduate Teacher Training Programme (GTTP) through the King Edward's Foundation too and I act as senior tutor.

Case study (cont'd)

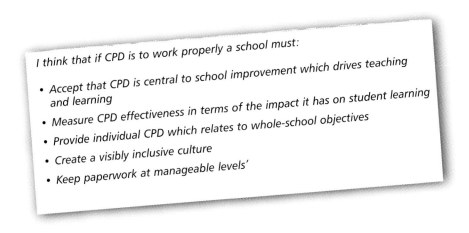

I think that if CPD is to work properly a school must:

- *Accept that CPD is central to school improvement which drives teaching and learning*
- *Measure CPD effectiveness in terms of the impact it has on student learning*
- *Provide individual CPD which relates to whole-school objectives*
- *Create a visibly inclusive culture*
- *Keep paperwork at manageable levels'*

CPD glossary

APL – Accreditation of Prior Learning – process whereby someone's previous achievements are counted towards a qualification

Cascading – passing on to colleagues information acquired at a course

GTTP – Graduate Teacher Training Programme. On the job training for graduates aged 24+. Provides CPD opportunities for existing staff in schools too

HEI – Higher Education Institution (eg a university)

INSET – In-service training. Usually a whole-school course or development activity

LPSH – Leadership Programme for Service Head Teachers. CPD programme provided for serving heads by National College for School Leadership

NPQH – National Professional Qualification for Headship. CPD programme for teachers aiming to become heads

Peer observation – Teachers of equal status observing each other's work and using it as a basis for constructive discussion

SCITT – School Centred Initial Teacher Training. On the job training for teachers, usually from other professions. Provides CPD opportunities for existing teachers in the schools because they help provide the training

SD – Staff Development. Another term for CPD

TASC – Teaching as A Second Career

Useful CPD organisations

- General Teaching Council (GTC England) **www.gtce.org.uk**
- General Teaching Council (GTC Wales) **www.gtcw.org.uk**
- British Educational Research Association (BERA) **www.bera.ac.uk**
- National Foundation for Educational Research (NFER) **www.nfer.ac.uk**
- TDA (Training and Development Agency for schools), formerly Teacher Training Agency **www.tda.gov.uk**
- Evidence-based Education UK **www.cemcentre.org/ebeuk**
- National College for School Leadership **www.ncsl.org.uk**
- Specialist Schools and Academies Trust **www.specialistschools.org.uk**

Subject organisations

- National Association for the Teaching of English **natehq@btconnect.com**
  www.nate.org.uk
- Association of Teachers of Mathematics **admin@atm.org.uk www.atm.org.uk**
- The Association for Science Education **info@ase.org.uk www.ase.org.uk**
- The Geographical Association **info@geography.org.uk www.geography.org.uk**
- The Historical Association **enquiry@history.org.uk www.history.org.uk**
- National Association of Music Educators **www.name2.org.uk**
- National Society for Education in Art and Design **www.nsead.org.uk**
- The Professional Council for Religious Education **retoday@retoday.org.uk**
  www.pcfre.org.uk
- The Association for Language Learning **info@all-languages.org.uk**
  www.all-languages.org.uk
- The Physical Education Association of the United Kingdom
  enquiries@pea.uk.com www.pea.uk.com
- Association for ICT Teachers and Coordinators **www.acitt.org.uk**
- The Design Technology Association **http://web.data.org.uk**

More sources of CPD information

- TeacherNet source of online information set up by DfES to provide CPD for teachers **www.teachernet.gov.uk**
- VTC Virtual Teacher Centre. Government interactive website providing support and learning for teachers **www.vtc.ngfl.gov.uk**
- *CPD Update*. Print newsletter. 10 issues per year. Optimus Publishing **www.optimuspub.co.uk**
- Connect. Online GTCE network for CPD coordinators. Termly electronic newsletters. **cpdnetwork@gtce.org.uk** 020 7841 2908 **www.gtce.org.uk/networks/connect**
- Centre for British Teachers **www.cfbt.com**
- Teachers TV **www.teachers.tv**
- TeacherFirst Online CPD and support package for schools **www.education-quest.com**

About the author

Susan Elkin

Susan Elkin MA, BA (Hons), Cert Ed, MCIJ is a journalist, writer and former secondary school teacher.

She writes on education topics for *Daily Mail, The Daily Telegraph, SecEd, The Stage, The Music Teacher, PTA Magazine* and many other publications. She edited *CPD Update* from 2001-2005 and *Early Years Update, which she launched,* from 2002-2005.

Susan's books include *So You Really Want to Learn English* Books 1, 2 and 3, a student study guide and teacher resource pack on *To Kill a Mockingbird, 101 Essential Lists for Secondary Teachers* and 17 book-format reports for the Specialist Schools and Academies Trust.

During her time as an English teacher in five schools and three LEAs, Susan held a number of senior posts including head of department, head of year, head of upper school and CPD coordinator.

Order Form

Your details

Name _____

Position _____

School _____

Address _____

_____

_____

Telephone _____

Fax _____

E-mail _____

VAT No. (EC only) _____

Your Order Ref _____

Please send me:

		No. copies
The CPD	Pocketbook	
_____	Pocketbook	
_____	Pocketbook	
_____	Pocketbook	
_____	Pocketbook	

Order by Post

Teachers' Pocketbooks

Laurel House, Station Approach
Alresford, Hants. SO24 9JH UK

Order by Phone, Fax or Internet

Telephone: +44 (0)1962 735573
Facsimile: +44 (0)1962 733637
E-mail: sales@teacherspocketbooks.co.uk
Web: www.teacherspocketbooks.co.uk

Pocketbooks

Teachers' Titles:		Selected Management Titles:	
A-Z of Educational Terms	Fundraising for Schools	Appraisals	Meetings
Accelerated Learning	Head of Department's	Assertiveness	Mentoring
Behaviour Management	ICT in the Classroom	Career Transition	Motivation
Coaching & Reflecting	Inclusion	Challenger's	Negotiator's
Creative Teaching	Learning to Learn	Coaching	NLP
CPD	Managing Workload	Communicator's	Openers & Closers
Dyslexia	Primary Headteacher's	Controlling Absenteeism	People Manager's
Form Tutor's	Primary Teacher's	Decision-making	Performance Management
	Promoting Your School	Developing People	Personal Success
	Pupil Mentoring	Discipline	Positive Mental Attitude
	Secondary Teacher's	Emotional Intelligence	Presentations
	Stop Bullying	Empowerment	Problem Behaviour
	Teaching Assistant's	Energy & Well-being	Project Management
	Trips & Visits	Icebreakers	Resolving Conflict
		Impact & Presence	Succeeding at Interviews
		Influencing	Self-managed Development
		Interviewer's	Stress
		Leadership	Teamworking
		Learner's	Thinker's
		Managing Budgets	Time Management
		Managing Change	Trainer's
		Managing Your Appraisal	Vocal Skills

Inclusion is…

 Building an
Inclusive Ethos

 Formulating an
Inclusion Policy

 Managing
Inclusion

 Inclusive
Classrooms –
Planning & Teaching

 Inclusive Learning
Environments

 Evaluating
Inclusion

 Further
Information

Further
Information

Rights, legislation and guidance

This section is intended as an at-a-glance summary. Do refer to the original legislation and guidance when writing policies or making decisions.

The Salamanca Statement (1994)

The Salamanca Statement was written at a world conference on special educational needs organised by UNESCO. Ninety-two governments were represented.

Inclusive schooling is the most effective means for building solidarity between children with special needs and their peers. Inclusive schools must recognise and respond to the diverse needs of their students, accommodating both different styles and rates of learning and ensuring quality education to all through appropriate curricula, organisational arrangements, teaching strategies, resource use and partnerships with their communities.

Rights, legislation and guidance

UN Convention on the rights of the Child (1990) Article 29

The education of the child shall be directed to:

- The development of the child's personality, talents and mental and physical abilities to their fullest potential
- The development of respect for the child's parents, his or her own cultural identity, language and values, for the national values of the country in which the child is living, the country from which he or she may originate, and for civilisations different from his or her own
- The preparation of the child for responsible life in a free society, in the spirit of understanding, peace, tolerance, equality of sexes, and friendship among all peoples, ethnic, national and religious groups and persons of indigenous origin

Rights, legislation and guidance

The SEN and Disability Act

There is a range of legislation and guidance which applies to students with disabilities:

- The Disability Discrimination Act (2002)
- The SEN framework

These encompass three complementary strands:

- The disability discrimination duties
- The SEN framework
- The planning duties

The legislation describes a disabled person as someone who has a physical or mental disability which has an effect on his or her ability to carry out normal day to day activities. That effect must be substantial, adverse and long term. This definition of physical and mental disability includes sensory impairments; severe disfigurement; hidden disabilities such as learning difficulties, dyslexia, mental illness; and physical conditions like diabetes or epilepsy.

Rights, legislation and guidance

The disability discrimination duties

The SEN and Disability Act identifies two duties which all schools must fulfil:

- A duty not to treat disabled students less favourably, without justification, than their non-disabled peers
- A duty to make reasonable adjustments to ensure that students who are disabled are not put at a substantial disadvantage in comparison to students who are not disabled

Schools are required to take steps to identify and to make provision for disability. These steps must be informed and timely and must anticipate pupils' needs. The onus is on the school and not on the parents or the student. All aspects of school life, eg admissions, educational provision and exclusions are covered by these duties.

Rights, legislation and guidance

Disability discrimination and the SEN framework

There are two key concepts underpinning the duties in this legislation:

1. **Less favourable treatment** is about denying a pupil access to the school or any activity or facility on the grounds of their disability. You will have to justify less favourable treatment and demonstrate that you have made reasonable adjustments.

2. **Reasonable adjustments** are changes to practice, organisation or policy that anticipate the needs of the disabled pupils so that they are not placed at substantial disadvantage in comparison to their peers. Reasonable adjustment does not cover the provision of additional aids or services, which are accessed through the SEN framework, or physical alterations to buildings, which are covered through the planning duties.

The Special Educational Needs Code of Practice (2001) provides guidance on the responsibilities of schools to identify and provide for students with special educational needs. Governing bodies are responsible for ensuring that schools have regard to the Code of Practice in carrying out their duties towards these pupils.

Rights, legislation and guidance

Disability discrimination and the planning duty

Schools are required to have a plan which describes how accessibility for disabled students will increase three things:

- **Physical access**, through improving the physical environment of school so that disabled students can take advantage of education and associated services provided by schools, eg ramps, handrails and lifts, ICT equipment, specialist desks and chairs

- **Access to the curriculum**, through staff information and training, improved classroom organisation and whole school organisation such as timetabling

- **Access to written information**, through considering the use of handouts, timetables and newsletters and looking at alternative provision including braille, large print, audio tapes and oral delivery of information

Rights, legislation and guidance

The Race Relations (Amendment) Act 2000

This describes the requirement for schools to:
- promote racial equality
- promote good race relations
- eliminate unlawful racial discrimination

Racism and lack of cultural understanding exist in all communities whether they are culturally mixed or not. Under the Act, **all** schools should have a written race equality policy and an action plan which shows how the policy is being put into practice.

A senior member of staff should lead on the monitoring of the policy and action plan, consulting and involving groups within and outside school. The policy statement for race equality should cover your school's aims and values, arrangements for policy planning and review, and for implementing the policy. The policy should be linked to the action plan, which includes time-scales for reviewing and evaluating impact.

Rights, legislation and guidance

Every Child Matters: Change for Children

Every Child Matters: Change for Children is a new approach to the well-being of children and young people from birth to age 19.
The Government's aim is for every child, whatever their background or their circumstances, to have the support they need to:

- Be healthy
- Stay safe
- Enjoy and achieve
- Make a positive contribution
- Achieve economic well-being

This means that the organisations involved with providing services to children - from hospitals and schools, to police and voluntary groups - will be teaming up in new ways, sharing information and working together, to protect children and young people from harm and help them achieve what they want in life. Children and young people will have far more say about issues that affect them as individuals and collectively.'
http://www.everychildmatters.gov.uk/aims

Bibliography

Understanding the Development of Inclusive Schools
by M. Ainscow.
Published by Routledge Falmer (1999)

Inclusive Education: International Voices on Disability and Justice
by K. Ballard (Editor).
Published by Falmer Press (1999)

'On Sheep and Goats and School Reform'
by R. Barth in Phi Delta Kappan 68 (4) (1986)

Index for Inclusion
by T. Booth & M. Ainscow.
Published by CSIE (2002)

Statutory Code of Practice on the Duty to Promote Race
CRE (2002)

The National Curriculum
DfEE (1999)

SEN and Disability Act, 2001
DfES (2001)

Special Educational Needs Code of Practice
DfES (2001)

Schools and Special Needs
by A. Dyson & A. Millward.
Published by Paul Chapman (2000)

Special Educational Needs & School Improvement
by J. Gross & A. White.
Published by David Fulton (2003)

Disability and Discrimination Act
(1995) HMSO

Bibliography

Special Educational Needs and Disability Act (2001)
HMSO (2001)

Professional Learning Communities
by S. Hord.
Published by Southwest Educational Development Laboratory (1997)

Framework for Inspecting Schools
Ofsted (2003)

Evaluating Educational Inclusion Guidance for Inspectors and Schools
Ofsted (2000)

Reinventing Government
by D. Osborne & T. Gaebler.
Published by Addison Wesley (1992)

Planning, Teaching and Assessing the Curriculum for Pupils with Learning Difficulties
QCA (2001)

Inclusive Schools: Inclusive Society-Race and Identity on the Agenda
by R. Richardson & A. Wood.
Published by Trentham Books (1999)

Accelerated Learning
by C. Rose.
Published by Dell (1995)

The Salamanca Statement and Framework for Action on Special Needs Education
UNESCO (1994)

UN Convention on the Rights of the Child
UNICEF (1989)

About the authors

Niki Elliot
B.Sc, PGCE, M.A. (Education).

Niki has over 20 years' experience in the field of inclusion in schools and LAs. She has co-ordinated special educational needs in two secondary schools, both of which had specialist SEN resources. She has held senior management positions in a special school, where she was responsible for the primary phase, and a secondary school where she was responsible for inclusion. Niki was principal adviser for inclusion in a local authority and has worked as an independent consultant and an Ofsted inspector. She is now a principal lecturer at Sheffield Hallam University continuing to specialise in inclusion, integrated working and evaluation in schools.

You can contact Niki at n.elliot@shu.ac.uk

About the authors

Elaine Doxey

Cert. Ed, B.Ed, Mathematics Diploma, Certificate SEN co-ordination.

Elaine retired in September 2007. She was formerly an LA advisory teacher for inclusion with responsibility for special educational needs. Elaine previously taught in primary schools where in addition to class teacher she had responsibility for co-ordinating special educational needs, key stage 2 and maths. She has also undertaken consultancy and advisory work in promoting circle time and positive behaviour.

Val Stephenson

M.Ed (Special and Inclusive Education), Advanced Diploma in Guidance and Counselling in Schools.

Val is a Senior Lecturer in Primary Education. She has taught in a wide range of primary schools and early years settings, both as class teacher and in senior management positions. A former advisory teacher for inclusion, with particular responsibility for able, gifted and talented pupils, she has also undertaken consultancy and advisory work, specialising in diversity. In her current role she pursues her particular research interests in the areas of dual and multiple exceptionality, and learning disabilities.

Order form

Your details

Name _____

Position _____

School _____

Address _____

_____

_____

Telephone _____

Fax _____

E-mail _____

VAT No. (EC only) _____

Your Order Ref _____

Please send me:

		No. copies
Inclusion	Pocketbook	☐
_____	Pocketbook	☐
_____	Pocketbook	☐
_____	Pocketbook	☐
_____	Pocketbook	☐

Order by Post

**Teachers'
Pocketbooks**

Laurel House, Station Approach
Alresford, Hants. SO24 9JH UK

Order by Phone, Fax or Internet

Telephone: +44 (0)1962 735573
Facsimile: +44 (0)1962 733637
E-mail: sales@teacherspocketbooks.co.uk
Web: www.teacherspocketbooks.co.uk